Regaining
Consciousness
in the Western World

Regaining Consciousness in the Western World

Radical Essays on the Human Experience

Reverend Maya Sarada Devi

Dawn Rose Press
Sebastopol, California

Regaining Consciousness in the Western World

© 1990 by Maya Sarada Devi

ISBN 0-9265744-0-6

Published by
Dawn Rose Press
12470 Fiori Lane
Sebastopol, California 95472

Cover photo by David Licht
Cover and book design by Paula Morrison
Typeset by Campaigne & Associates

Manufactured in the United States of America

Library of Congress Catalog Card Number 90–082069

For my husband and best friend, Chris, whose love, encouragement and patience made this book possible.

And for Jillian, Caitlin, and Dawn Rose whose innocent, trusting faces inspire dreams of a better world.

Contents

Foreword xi

Preface xiii

I. Hello, Everyone 1

II. The Form of Essence and
the Essence of Form 9

III. What Do You Want? 15

IV. Who *Is* God, Anyway? 21

V. The Blind Leading the Blind 27

VI. This Is Hell! 33

VII. What Are You Saying? 39

VIII. For Our Children 45

IX. Aborting Abortion 53

X. The Most *Misunderstood* Word
in the English Language 57

XI. So, What Do We Do *Now*? 61

XII. Welcome! 65

Afterword 67

Glossary 69

Bibliography 71

Do not concern yourself with the world around you. Consider that you *are* the world. How would you have yourself be?

Foreword

Many of us are inspired by what we have read, lectures we have heard, passionate messages from the pulpit, and by our very own lucid dreams. There are many people walking around our planet who are divinely inspired and who share a vision for the world that is quite different from the world we know today. Perhaps the biggest question is how can we *integrate* our ideals, visions, and dreams for a joyous world into the lives we live *now*. What can we do as individuals which will actually cause shifts in the consciousness of the whole human planet?

Most of us excuse ourselves from personal responsibility for the problems we face each day, instead blaming society, political leaders, or historical events. But our societies are made up of individual people who have agreed to participate in and support a particular group life experience. And if this way of living is not meeting the real needs of the participants, perhaps it is time to consider alternatives. The probability of a group meeting among all members of our society is very small. However, we *can* communicate our desires to eachother* quite clearly by personally *living* the way we believe is most supportive to our health and well-being, physically, emotionally, and spiritually.

---

*In the English language, the words *each other* are separate. This is not accidental, but in fact illustrates our feeling of separateness from one another. I choose now to bring us together as one.

Of what value is our human experience if it is not joyous, spontaneous, sensitive, intuitive, and actively creative? Why even bother with a life that is passive, resigned to a grim "reality"? We have tried numbing out with alcohol, drugs, marijuana, and by cutting ourselves off from our emotions. We go to therapists to recover from these addictions, but why bother becoming sensitive and aware again? The culture that we live in does not support our being this way. In order to live a way of life which supports love among all people and continued vibrant health for all life forms on the planet, one must actually live outside the *consciousness* of his culture. Thankfully, many brave and committed individuals already do. These people have chosen empowerment through personal responsibility, ongoing commitment to their ideals, and manifestation of their dreams through their own perseverance.

When more than half the members of our culture choose to create a more sane way of living, refusing to participate in the unsupportive value systems on which our culture is based, our culture will cease to be. Very confrontive indeed!

The seeds for an entirely new culture are already sprouting, one which combines the wisdom of ancient peoples with our own fresh imagination and creativity. Those who have invested the whole of their energies in a culture based on competition, economics, imperialism, and high technology will feel understandably threatened, defensive, and angry. A new value system completely undermines the old one, and confronts those who stubbornly cling to the very beliefs which have prevented them from having the ecstatic experience they were born to have.

Preface

What I attempt to offer in this collection of essays is wisdom which guides us as we experience human form. It is not within my ability, nor is it appropriate for me to discuss the experiences we will have after the human experience. As a being in human form, I, myself, am capable of drawing into my awareness only that wisdom which I am ready to receive and apply in a meaningful way. The wisdom which I have called for to guide my own process of enlightenment is that which I offer you now.

Much "channeled" material has been published in years past. And some of what I write will seem quite similar. The messages come from the same collective consciousness that we all share. All who are able to tap into our collective consciousness and bring forth wisdom for those who cannot should be acknowledged for making the effort of sharing this wisdom. Words of wisdom can never be repeated too many times, nor in too many ways. Once fully received, they will be acknowledged by all for their vital importance in our lives.

The messages offered within the following essays are true to the degree which the written word can convey truth. The intention of these writings is to catalyze the remembering of the true self, the God within each of us, the life blood shared by us all. True understanding is the opening of the heart, rather than the exercising of the mind. Therefore, it is my true desire that the words which follow will be recognized in such a profound way as to cause a shift in consciousness, an opening of the heart, and the beginning of a new awareness of ourselves and of eachother.

If our world is in turmoil, there must be a reason. Is it simply human nature which predisposes us to relate to eachother as opponents? Or do we purposely oppose eachother in an attempt to define who and what we are? Will the solutions to our world problems be found as we make changes within our existing human systems, or must we abandon these systems altogether and begin a new way of relating to eachother and to our earth? Perhaps world peace, personal happiness for every living being on our beautiful planet, *is* possible. Maybe the answers to our questions come, not in changing the form of things, but in changing the essence—the consciousness—of human experience. It is of value to consider that happiness and peace for the whole of the human planet may occur, not as a result of group decisions and politics, but as a result of millions and millions of personal commitments.

I

Hello, Everyone

I am a minister. I am a college dropout, a wife, a mother of three, a child from a dysfunctional family. I go to the grocery store like everyone else. I drive a car. I think everyday thoughts just like you do. But sometimes there is a shift of consciousness within me where everything is profoundly different. Nothing seems the same at all. I am filled with this overwhelming and wonderful feeling of love, not just for my husband and children—but for everyone and everything. It's quite remarkable, really. I cannot predict when and if it will happen to me. But in recent years, it seems like I am in this state of awareness about half the time. I hope someday to be this way all the time. And when this shift within me takes place, I am filled with what I can only call a higher knowing. When I am in this state of awareness, everything seems so simple and so clear to me. The questions that have plagued mankind for centuries seem suddenly so silly. When I am in my state of higher knowing I realize that the reason humans have not found answers to their questions is simply because the wrong questions are being asked.

How do I know the things I know? How can I make such bold assertions? I can only answer these questions by offering that you join me in this state of consciousness, even for a little while, and discover your own higher knowing. When one looks at life through the eyes of his higher vision, he has the wisdom, perspective, and understanding of one who stands at the top of a tall mountain on a clear day. The vista cannot be described to companions below. They must go and see for themselves.

Since I was a very small child I have had visions. I have seen and heard things that I did not understand. I was told that I had a vivid imagination. I was told that I was a liar. So I decided at a young age never to tell anyone about what I saw and knew. But now I understand that metaphorically it was my destiny to climb the mountain and return to share a vision with the human world. The vision is one of a world at peace. And what I have come to know is that the vision is a very real future that we can choose for ourselves, first as individuals and ultimately as a human planet. And so I write this book. One of the ironies is that those who are brave enough to read it probably could have written it themselves. Those among us who need this book most will probably never want to read it. Therefore, one of the great secrets of life is to give yourself fully to an endeavor, and not feel a need for any particular outcome. A big sense of humor is the perfect balance to a loving heart. And now I surrender to my higher knowing and begin.

It is my greatest honor and my duty to address you today, those brothers and sisters who have borne themselves into human form for the ecstatic human experience. And I address you as one who loves you profoundly and totally. I was born for this moment, the moment when I would know truth in such a profound, all-encompassing way that I am able to serve as a messenger of all that would bring happiness and peace to my beloved human family.

I bring an offering for all who dare to dream that there is more to life than what they have thus far experienced. I dream that in this life experience, my offerings of wisdom may catalyze the integration of religion and science. It is also my hope that I may catalyze a new recognition of the truth within *all* the teachings handed down from the beginning of human form, teachings in every language all over the world.

You are unhappy. You have set aside your purpose and your true destiny. You have forgotten your true natures, and instead have been drawn into the illusion that your bodies are the beginning and end of your identity and being. It is no wonder that you busy yourselves in pursuit of physical things. Great misunderstanding and the loss of the true memory have caused the painful belief that wealth and success are found in the personal accumulation of physical forms which please the senses. Ultimately, the beautiful physical environment we manifested when we took form can only be fully enjoyed as a mutual, shared experience for us all. Division between us according to the current belief in "ownership" of land, food, water, and air only delays real human happiness. True and lasting happiness begins with the sudden all-encompassing realization by each member of the human family that we are truly all limbs of one body, that we cannot find our true selves until we recognize that everyone is us and we are everyone. In truth there is no separation. Only the illusion of separation exists in the dream of a human family asleep. And as new energies take form to aid in the awakening, they are lulled one after another into a deep sleep, hypnotically drawn, as well, into the dream of fear and separation.

We humans are limbs of the same body, flowers of the same plant, thoughts of the same mind, words from the same song. A limb cannot function without being part of the body. A flower cannot grow without the plant. Understanding is not found by one thought alone, but through the harmonious gathering of many thoughts. And one word will never a song make.

The hurdle we must jump is in the surrendering, the letting go of who and what we think we are, our self-importance, our personal ambitions. What ultimate value do they have, if it is not for the benefit of all? The awakening comes as humility. It comes as a flood of tears, a sudden realization that we had forgotten who we really are. It comes as a rushing river of remembering God. It knocks us over, so great is the impact. We look upon another face, and we see such texture and beauty, such potential, such depth. We are moved to tears again. We want to touch everything. The tree branches, the leaves, the damp cold earth. It is suddenly sacred to us. How could we not have felt this way before? The awakening is the coming alive in our sacred bodies. Emotions flood through us, our skin vibrates with sensation as we step near any and all forms of life.

We drink in the deliciousness, the realness, the truth of being alive in physical form. The experience is all-encompassing; we are overwhelmed by the beauty, the perfect organization of all the forms, the repeated patterns from the lightning in the sky to the branches of the huge oak tree, the river fingering into streams, the arteries and veins in our own bodies.

The air we breathe has a taste all its own. We become painfully aware of the inappropriateness of dirtying our air environment. Nothing is important enough to sacrifice the sweetness we breathe in and out. All growing, living, vibrating energies feel so much a part of us, that we begin to understand that we are not separate from them, in fact we are not separate from anything. Suddenly searching for

4

God seems like a meaningless concept. You recognize that God *is* you, is *everything*. And you are everything. You and all life are one body, one life, one God! When the truth of life becomes *your* truth, you step out into the world with the love, the patience, and the wisdom of a great master. And the awakening has begun.

In natural healthy living, an individual is a fully vibrating, radiating, alive energy. He is sensing and intuiting what is most appropriate in each moment. He is always in contact with an inner awareness which guides him. And he trusts this awareness absolutely and without question. All choices and movements are guided by his own inner awareness. Emotions are an important part of his awareness and he allows himself to feel them fully. He is able to ask for what he wants and takes full responsibility for his own happiness. As a powerful creative energy, it is impossible for him to be anyone's victim because he is free to experience life any way he chooses.

II

The Form of Essence
and the Essence of Form

Physical form was dreamed up when the desire for new experience and expression became strong enough to manifest. In fact it was we who invented physical form. In bodies we can make love, and experience the delights of taste, smell, sound, vision, and touch. The manifestation of physical form, like all new creative directions, brought trials, challenges, and inevitably wisdom. Physical bodies were limiting in ways that were suffocating to some, but the sensuous, delicious, intoxicating experience of the five physical senses, and the exhilarating experience of the physical life cycles were delightfully alluring. And so we are here. We enjoy the breathtaking mountains, the peaceful shore, the mysterious deserts, and the dreamy rain forests. We relish in the change of the seasons, and the changes in eachother. What is dearer than the experience of suckling a newborn, or making passionate love with your mate? What is more delicious than the sweet juice of fruit running down your chin, the smell of a warm fire in the winter, a bicycle race, climbing a tall mountain to savor the vista at the top, a hot cup of cinnamon tea and a soft, warm blanket, or a tiny kitten curled up sleeping on your lap? And so we are here. What exhilaration in designing and creating and building! What entertainment in watching the natural world all around us, a crescendo of singing, playing, building, running, jumping, cuddling, and loving!

And so we have chosen to experience physical form. It is lush, beautiful, fulfilling. Why, then, you ask, is there so much pain in the world?

If one is to address the pain, the confusion, the anger, the power-struggling, the aggression, and apparent suffering, one must begin with the Fall. What precipitated the loss of our higher awareness, I do not consciously remember at this time. When did the Fall occur? A long time ago.

What can be said is that there was a split between essence and form, between matter and spirit, between the creator and what was created. It is that we can no longer hear our own voices. We are operating without our true "brain," so to speak. It is the physical brain that we now rely on, an organ created to help our bodies function in space, not an organ of higher purpose and creative manifestation. The body is form. That which inhabits the body is essence. As happy humans, we are the balance of both. Lacking such balance, we are lost wanderers, struggling and unhappy.

We have directed so much of our energies through the physical brain that we have become analytical, scientific, rational, and intellectual. We separate and categorize, and dissect and analyze and still we can't remember who we are.

Science originally began as play. We played with our environment, watched, enjoyed, and wondered at the miracle of all life forms. We delighted in observing and sharing all that we saw before us. When we abandoned our higher awareness, science became the search for greater understanding and meaning using our physical brains alone. The human brain was designed as part of an organic mechanism of perception and response to the physical world. Scientific study, even through the highly developed physical human brain, can never hope to arrive at the essence of life.

And so we have now a world in which science, intellectual understanding, dissection and categorization of the human being and of the world have replaced attempts at reconnecting to our higher wisdom. Talk has replaced listening. Mechanized cities have paved over the natural beauty that was our sacred home. The constant search for physical gratification and the hoarding of resources has replaced shared ecstasy in the abundant pristine world. Some humans are fat and some humans are starving for food. Some humans need castles to hold all that they have struggled so hard to accumulate, while others wish only for a roof over their heads. Some humans have a different body covering for each day of the year, while others shiver with cold. Some humans are afraid of losing their vast holdings, while others feel victimized and angry at having so little.

It is a world vibrating with anger and fear, guilt and shame. It is a world ripening for war: the war that will end the human experience, the war that will end the enjoyment of merging form with essence.

Nuclear war may be the only way to have a "meeting of the minds." Out of body, we flow right back to our source. If it is true that the only way for us to remember our true identity and purpose is to create such violence that our physical forms are completely destroyed, then so be it. World war is a perfectly valid, if drastic, means to reuniting with eachother in spirit.

I am perfectly willing to go along with a majority vote on this, as long as we are all clear enough about what we are *really* doing to make an informed choice.

There is a fine line between sculpting and controlling. Sculpting is an endeavor of love. Controlling is an expression of fear.

III

What Do You Want?

As a minister, counselor, spiritual teacher and healer, I have had the privilege of working very intimately with individuals in great life pain. In my experience, I have found that ultimately each person really wants the same things:

1. Recognition of her own identity as being more than her physical body.
2. Intimacy, honesty, and love with other human beings.
3. A sense of his life purpose (reason for being in physical form at this time).
4. Uninterrupted connection with God.

So it seems rather odd that so much human energy is invested in the building and maintaining of a life experience which includes little or none of the things we really yearn for. Our lives are enmeshed in high technology, mass production, traffic, pollution, and noise. We see hundreds of people each day, but hardly notice them. At work we treat people in a less than sensitive way, justifying our behavior with the phrase "business is business."

In Woody Allen's movie "Love and Death," Don Francisco's impersonator says, "I've got all the details worked out. Now if I can just think of the main points." As hilarious as this scene was in the movie, it's quite sobering to recognize that we suffer the same dilemma in our own lives. We have all the details worked out: the job, the mortgage, the car, the appliances, the wife, the kids, the sports page, and our favorite t.v. show. We can look around us at all the things we own, the photo albums of all the trips we've taken, the parties we've had, the memories of a busy life with more memories in the making. We can feel satisfied, perhaps, that we have "more than most," more than the other guy—the one who asked us for some spare change so he could get a cup of coffee—*but are we happy*?

We have been so busy with the details of our lives that we have forgotten the main points. Considering the meaning and purpose of our own human experience is an activity we don't have time for. We are so consumed by the day-to-day struggle we know as "reality," that we hardly pause to question the belief systems which prejudice our very perceptions about who and what we are. We have closed our eyes to our own higher awareness, and closed our ears to the voice of greater wisdom within us. We no longer feel our own life blood pulsing within us—within all of us. We no longer feel the uncontainable joy of each new day, the wonder of looking into eachother's eyes, and the happiness of loving eachother. We no longer consider ourselves to be sacred beings, and therefore nothing else is sacred to us, either. And so we relate to ourselves, eachother, and our world in a way which causes us great physical and emotional distress. We relate to all life in a way which does not support its continuation as we know it. It is only natural that we are suffering the symptoms of what we are doing to ourselves.

But rather than address our physical and emotional pain as potent information for the whole human family, we seek individual treatment for our symptoms—and go right back to the way of being which caused these symptoms in the first place.

As powerful co-creators of the human experience, it is our responsibility to clearly envision what we want for ourselves, for eachother, and for our world. Our pain comes from living in the illusion that we are helpless victims of a harsh "reality." We have listened to and acted on our human intellect—rather than trusting the gentle voice of our higher wisdom. And so, we have created painful life experiences for ourselves.

It seems very clear that we really *do* need the same four things in order to be happy. But the irony is that this, too, is an illusion. The four ingredients to happiness listed at the beginning of this essay are actually one truth stated four different ways. And in this same way, the essays in this book are simply one message stated many ways. The basis of ongoing vibrant health is simply happiness. And for most of us, real happiness—the kind of ongoing joyous, delicious shared human experience where every living being and every precious moment is received as a sacred, beautiful gift—is something that has never even crossed our human minds.

Fear is confusion. Love is clarity. Decisions made from fear will always bring more confusion. Decisions born from love will bring even greater clarity.

IV

Who *Is* God, Anyway?

All over the world, human beings are worshipping a God which they consider to be separate from themselves, somewhere up in the clouds. For the most part, those who pray and participate in daily or weekly rituals are simply following in the footsteps of their ancestors, going through the motions without having a personal mystical experience. Christian doctrine teaches us that human beings are made in the image of God. And this is indeed true, but not in the sense that God is a human-looking being up in the sky with whom we will meet some fateful day. In truth, we *are* God—not as individuals—but as the whole of all life in and out of form.

One can say that everything a sculptor creates, she makes in her own image. The sculpture may not be made in the image of the artist's physical body, but nevertheless it is made in her own image, the image of the essence of her being.

The essence of our being is a shared essence which has manifested in many different physical forms and personalities. We are like music wanting to play—so we create an orchestra—one musician for each instrument needed to have a full musical expression. God is the music and we are the musicians we created before we were we, back when together we knew ourselves simply as I.

Certainly our human minds cannot begin to grasp the infinite. As physical beings, our awareness is directed at things which seem finite. We experience life as something which begins and finally ends, like the years and the seasons. From a physical point of view, we perceive everything in finite terms. "Nothing goes on forever." It is surprising that the English language even contains the words *infinite* and *forever*. These are vague notions, at best. And in the same way, that which we call *God* is an even vaguer notion, as vague as the awareness of our own true identities.

In fact, everything *does* go on forever. Because God goes on forever, and God is the name we give to *all that is*, the great *everything*. There is simply nothing which exists that is not God. Therefore, since God is a never-ending event, and God is everything: *everything* is a never-ending event. Only the forms change. Only the shapes, the colors, and the faces change.

It is our confusion between form and essence which causes this great identity crisis. If we cut ourselves off from our awareness of the essence of life, then we have cut off our ability to perceive our own essence as well. It is no wonder that we confuse our essence with our forms. If we are a society of beings who believe that we *are* nothing more than our physical forms, then that event which we call "death" would naturally seem like quite a threat to everything that we have come to know and love —the end of our connection with the world, with our loved ones, with nature, and with God. If we have no sense of our own infinity, then we have no sense of God. And until each of us really understands that she *is* God, not by herself—but as a whole with all that exists with her—she will have no understanding of her own identity.

So, rest assured that most everyone you meet in the Western World is suffering from a paralyzing identity crisis. This, alone, is reason enough to have compassion for one another.

Those who resist us actually help define us. Those who oppose us are the very contrast we need in order to see ourselves clearly. Therefore, are opponents really enemies? Or are they friends of a different color?

V

The Blind Leading the Blind

Human language and culture are virtually the same thing. Language is the set of symbols, spoken or written, which allows us to relay our experiences to eachother. Culture is the shared belief system which determines what we believe about our experiences, and therefore determines our perception. Language is the sharing with eachother of our perceptions. Since language and culture occur simultaneously, the symbols and meanings found within language will always be an expression of the cultural belief system. Therefore, the opportunity for unbiased perception, free of cultural conditioning, is severely limited. The language of each culture represents only those perceptions shared by the culture. Any ideas or perceptions beyond the scope of the language are simply not expressed.

Only very young children, who have not yet assimilated the language of their parents, have free, innocent, unbiased and therefore true life experience. Once they begin to speak, children find themselves unable to communicate the true depth, texture, and meaning of their experiences, so limited is the scope of the language. Because the sensitive, intuitive experiences of children are not acknowledged by the culture, there are no symbols through which a child may express them. Over time, a child loses touch with the perceptions he is unable to share, as he assimilates the language and limited perception of the culture in which he is raised.

Symbols can only hint at essence. Intimate contact without the interference of written or spoken language is true communication. Sadly, humans have become so disconnected from eachother, so fearful of intimacy, that communication of such sacredness is rare. The basis for such communication must be established first, in the form of utmost respect and unconditional acceptance of one another. Certainly, everyone wants to be loved. If there is an energy of judgment in the world, few will be courageous enough to share the truth of their own beings. Of course, most people don't even know the truth of their own beings.

It is interesting to consider the root of the tremendous self-rejection, harsh judgment of others, and feelings of fear, anger and betrayal. People believe they cannot trust eachother.*

Imagine for a moment a blind man without any tools for his own mobility. Would he seek out another blind person like himself to be his guide? Or would he have greater trust in the guidance of a sighted person—one with greater perception than himself? I believe he would prefer the sighted guide, not trusting the perceptions of his blind associate any more than he trusts his own.

---

*The deep feelings of anger and disappointment we have for ourselves and for eachother stem from the recognition that we are all too fearful to seek out what we know at the core of our being is possible. We have betrayed ourselves and eachother by surrendering our creative power to our fear of the unknown and our fear of being alone. Man has sacrificed his own joy, the fulfilling of his personal dream, by choosing to stay at home in the familiar house of his own fear.

I use this as a metaphor only, because loss of physical sight is unrelated to true perception. But for purposes of understanding, I ask you to imagine a world of humans with blindfolds on, none of them knowing how to remove them. They fumble through life looking for physical and social comforts, yet very few of them ever address what life would be like if they removed the blindfolds. Secretly, each of them knows that he can remove the blindfold and have the vision of a million sparkling rainbows. Each of them also secretly knows that *all* are capable of removing their blindfolds. But who wants to be the first one? Whomever is first takes the risk of being alone with his new vision, the risk of no longer being able to relate to the world in his comfortable, familiar way. He takes the risk that no one will want to relate to him, either. He would become too confrontive, a symbol by his very presence of the choice no one else is courageous enough to make. His blindfolded family and friends would feel uncomfortable around him. He would be completely misunderstood, hated in fact. He might have to live out his life alone with his joyous vision, sad that he had no one to share it with. And he might be so condemned by the society he longed to share his vision with, that perhaps they would kill him. But his words of joy, wisdom and love, the words of a true visionary who saw what all humans were born to see, and knew what all humans were meant to know—would echo long after he transcended human form, leaving a trail for those courageous enough to follow.

Living a lifetime is like reading a book. Can we really enjoy the story if we are busy worrying about what we will do when we finish it?

VI

This is Hell!

We are told that if we do not save ourselves, we will go to a place called "Hell," where this guy called "The Devil" lives, and that we will be "damned" forever and ever. Well, as ridiculous as this sounds to modern-thinking people, it's almost true.

The devil is that aspect of ourselves which does not believe we can free ourselves from our limitations, and who wants so much to be right that he will sabotage us at every opportunity. The devil is none other than the aspect of ourselves we must overcome, that insidious fear and self-rejection which tries to convince us that we don't deserve to be happy. The devil symbology also represents that callous, compassionless, angry judge that no one wants to face—and yet each of us does every day of our lives until we rid ourselves of him. It is the sword-bearing critic within each of us, lashing out at every opportunity to destroy our self-esteem.

If this heartless judge wins out, if we destroy our own feelings of self-worth by knocking ourselves down over and over again, never being able to measure up to our own impossible standards, we will believe that we have failed in every creative attempt we were brave enough to make—

and we will stop trying. This is when we are in hell. It is the house of our fear, our self-rejection, and our secret rejection of everyone else. It is the house where no one can "measure up." In this house we are painfully aware of everyone's shortcomings. Feelings of love, of compassion, of support for one another—these things are never found here.

Hell never exists by itself. Each of us must build such a place for herself. It is built with lack of faith in ourselves, and cemented with our own anger. It is a *dam* which holds us back from flowing with life, our own river-like essence held back—dammed up—stuck in the mire of judgment, cold anger, and the need to be right. And for as long as we choose to stay in this dark, lonely place—we are dammed, not *damned*, mind you—but *dammed*—just like a body of water trying to flow but meeting with a concrete wall. And just like a river that has been dammed up, our potential— our incredible creative forces—are held back, unused. What are we saving them for?

Those who have succumbed to their own inner devil, who have created hell for themselves, and who are dammed —need to focus the power of their own anger on that concrete wall and knock it right down. Releasing all the anger will unleash a dam of tears—and the river that is your life will flow freely again as it does in the healthy natural world.

You will never find a more condemning critic, nor a harsher judge than yourself. For none exists.

There is no frightening devil with horns who awaits you. You live with him right now. When you can love yourself so much, that even the devil within you is received as a vital and challenging link to your own development—you will never again need to retreat into self-rejection.

Being "damned" is actually a misnomer. In truth, it refers to being *dammed*. And this is a state of stuckness that you choose for yourself. The belief that you have no choice is just another aspect of this jail you build for yourself. If you believed you had a free choice about being there—you would probably move out of that space immediately. The jail of your own self-hatred and fear is of your own making and you are the jailer that holds the keys. Only when you can come up with a convincing reason that will change your own mind about yourself—will you allow yourself to be free.

(And the only compelling reason is love.)

Truth is something that is heard, rather than spoken. Listening with the heart, one hears the truth in all things. Listening with the mind, one hears falseness and confusion. It is natural, then, that those who perceive with their intellect are cynical, and those who perceive with love are at peace.

VII

What Are You Saying?

Words in the English language such as *random*, *accidental*, *happened*, *chance*, *luck*, and *fate* are perfect examples of a cultural belief system in which we regard ourselves as powerless victims of something we do not understand. Words like *birth life*, and *death* refer to the natural cycles in the physical world. But due to an absence of words describing the cycles of essential (whole self) development, one can infer that the culture does not believe such cycles exist. It is no wonder that inspirational messages of higher vision, purpose, and truth are met with looks of disbelief, or sighs of resignation. The people in the Western World live in a society of mixed messages. On the one hand, we have a language which makes no provision for a sense of ourselves beyond our physical body-identities. And on the other hand, we have religion which urges us to look deep into ourselves to find more. The culture and language do not support the acceptance of religious teachings. The very fact that they are called *religious* teachings, rather than *important life teachings* shows how our culture regards this vague notion of God as being something separate from reality.

Another example showing how our language and our perceptions are intertwined is the term "insanity," used to describe people who are found to be socially *unacceptable*. A person who is considered by our society to be *insane* is, in truth, a being who is too sensitive to participate in societal denial. This person lacks the courage and commitment, however, to seek and find the truth of his own being, and so remains in a state of anguish, self-hatred, and rejection of the society which is, itself, too blind to help him. And so he is labeled by his culture as being *insane*, a label which implies that his behavior is *not* representative of a greater, deeper, societal pain which he shares. The term "insanity" also implies the "patient's" lack of credibility. Other members of society no longer need to be confronted by his pain and confusion. Now that he is labeled *insane*, he is separate—not "one of us." This is how society deals with confrontation, ignores the calls for help from its own members, and perpetuates its own denial.

What is our definition of sanity? Is it having enough money to function in a money-oriented society? Is sanity the same as not making waves, not questioning the values upon which all our choices are made? I ask these questions after observing that those we think of as socially unacceptable are the poor, the homeless, and those who have turned to alcohol, drugs, or crime in response to a world which does not love them or want them. All humans need to be respected, honored, and loved. So here is the problem. Humans, for the most part, do not respect and honor eachother. Life in the Western World is a race for money and power. Money and power buy respect and love, so the stakes are very high.

In a world of concrete, metal, and glass, there are no streams to bathe in, no meadows to forage in, no trees to camp under for the night. In a world of fear, with police cars roaming the streets, it is hard to live a natural life without being arrested for loitering or trespassing. When our hard-earned money is taxed by our government, used to build weapons and to subsidize industries which are destroying our natural world—it is easy to feel hopeless. People who are hopeless simply stop caring. They turn to violence, an obvious way of expressing their feelings of having been betrayed by the rest of their fellows. They turn to alcohol or drugs, a quiet and desperate suicide for those who turn their anger against themselves.

Have you ever wondered about the thousands of people locked up in prisons in the United States? Why are they there? Did anyone ever listen to these people when they were young and innocent, asking only to be respected and cared about? Perhaps no one is courageous enough to admit the truth. Who among us can honestly say that he was raised by honest, caring parents who were completely devoted to eachother and to their children? Who among us can truthfully say that his entire family, his teachers, and his community lovingly received and nourished him to be a unique and powerful member of our society?

I ask you to consider that living in the modern world is so traumatic for all of us that we have all gone crazy. We have completely lost our minds. Insanity is found as much in corporate boardrooms as in sanitariums. If you want to know what insanity is, go see a toxic waste dump, or an old growth forest which has been clear-cut. If you want to see insanity, go to a supermarket and try to find anything to eat which hasn't been sprayed with toxic chemicals and refined until all the food value has been removed. Then go to a doctor's office and see the result of the way we live. If you want to see pure human folly, go watch the production of disposable plastic and styrofoam containers. Then go listen to city officials as they scratch their heads about

41

what to do with all the trash.

It is time to wonder about all the social misfits. How are they different from you? It seems that truly sensitive, honest beings cannot ignore what they know in their hearts. Gentle and peaceful men and women who regard all life as sacred, cannot participate in the destruction of our earth with a clear conscience. Gentle people cannot compete with other human beings for food, shelter, and clothing without feeling tremendous guilt and pain. How can we be happy while our fellows do without?

When a family seeks out a psychotherapist for help, the therapist helps the family members learn to relate to eachother in new supportive ways which will promote love and health. The entire human family has needed a psychotherapist for a very long time. We have tried to avoid responsiblity for our world by blaming our problems on eachother. We have tried to feel powerful by oppressing others. We have tried to feel rich by keeping others poor. We have tried to seem innocent by making others guilty. We have tried to feel free by incarcerating those we fear. Let's stop now and take a breath. It is time for us to change.

Life is easy, if you have no preferences.

VIII

For Our Children

From the moment they are born, our children are prepared for the "real" world. But what *is* the real world? What is *real*? Who among us has clearer vision, or a more open heart than a young child? How confused we are to imagine that it is the job of adults to teach children about the real world. Children are the only ones who can really see it! What ignorance we demonstrate when we force-feed our innocent, alive children the belief systems and values of a dysfunctional society. What folly, that we think our children need to be "toughened up" for the "real" world! Young children are sensitive, intuitive, unconditionally loving, and utterly honest. These are the very qualities we need to reclaim as a whole human planet, if we hope to create a world at peace.

The underlying theme of our society, and therefore of our educational system, is that there is not enough of everything for everyone. Without even questioning this belief, we anxiously prepare our children to be competitors in a world which we experience as being cold and cruel. Yet most of us would agree that inappropriate relationship to our environment and to eachother has created a lack of things we do need and an abundance of things we don't need. This is completely of our own doing. When we respect the natural world, it provides everything we need—including population control.

The belief that we are separate from eachother and from our environment is an illusion through which we perceive a need to compete for the trappings of happiness. The irony is that real happiness comes from shedding the illusion. The truth is that most of the world's "problems" are the result of relating to eachother as separate entities. You can imagine what problems might arise if you treated your own body parts as being separate from eachother. If you were cold, would you put on one sock—or one glove? Certainly not. Would you spend all your money on an item of clothing if you had no food to eat? Certainly not. Because we consider our bodies, not in terms of individual body parts needing attention, but as a whole living system —we are able to meet our body needs quite simply. In this way, if we consider the human world to be one body, in fact—the entire system of all life to be one body—our individual choices would reflect a shared intention for the health of the whole body of life.

You see, it is the consciousness which needs to change. It is unnecessary for us to consider the solutions to our world problems because as soon as we feel the truth of being one body together, our consciousness shifts completely and the solutions become obvious.

We have tried making rules about how to live, and enforcing them through punitive action. We have not created peace this way, because peace is a state of consciousness based on shared intention and global agreement. Therefore, political action directed at forcing other human beings to abide by our wishes will never bring us what we really want.

Ultimately, what humans *do* really want is love. And

until we start giving our love unconditionally and in a big way—to everyone—we will not have peace.

How, then, should we raise our children? As the question is asked, I immediately see a garden full of vegetables and flowers. And I see children tending the garden and singing songs. And I see a community, where the old and the young—and all those in between—are learning from eachother, working together, and sharing everything they have. The children do not have formal schooling, but they learn everything they need to know about respecting the natural world, and all fellow beings. Ancient art forms are being used again. World technology has changed. Nothing is produced which is "disposable." Plastics and styrofoam are things of the past. Transportation has changed completely. Automobiles are no longer being produced. Airplanes are no longer being used. The buildings in the large cities are being torn down. Trees are being planted. Old-age homes, day care for children of working mothers, government jobs, auto insurance, and taxes—are things only our grandfathers remember.

I could go on in detail to describe the beautiful and perfect world I have seen so clearly in my dreams over the years. Perhaps you have seen it too. By myself I cannot create such a place. And so I have written this book as a plea to all my fellows to stand up and be counted.

When the laws are written in our hearts, we will no longer need a government to enforce them. When peace is our highest priority, there will no longer be war. When our decisions are made from love, their result will be of benefit to all. When we begin trusting ourselves, we will no longer fear others.

We have a "civilization" which does not value sensitivity, but instead attempts to "toughen" children up in preparation for the "real" world. We have a society where love, honor, integrity, respect, and personal responsibility to a higher purpose are things we consider in our "spare time," instead devoting the bulk of our energy and personal power to the pursuit of money and all that money buys.

Our culture does not support joyous shared life experience. Instead, it fosters separation, competition, and fear. Competition is the result of a belief that there is not enough of everything for everyone. Competition, by its very nature, divides us along the lines of who has and who doesn't have. Competition plants the seeds of fear within us that cause us to lock our doors, to look over our shoulders, to teach our children to beware of "strangers." Trust is not a natural relationship between all beings. It is something reserved for the few who have proven to us that they can be trusted—that they are not going to take anything away from us.

It seems odd to me that psychiatrists, psychologists, and physicians work to *help* people adjust to living in a *dysfunctional* culture. This seems like a contradiction in terms. If the members of our society are suffering emotionally and physically, are we not participating in further denial by tranquilizing them, medicating them, or attempting to find individual solutions to a cultural problem?

We are encouraged to go to "therapists" who will help us resolve anger that we have at our parents and other people in our lives. Who *wouldn't* be angry at parents who teach them that they are nothing more than their bodies, accidentally popping into the world from who knows where, powerless victims of chance who can trust no one, and who must compete, not only for their physical sustenance, but for human love as well! If even the therapists, themselves, cannot see the bigger picture, how can they help the other members of their own society? Individual therapy is a bandaid approach to healing global amnesia. We can talk about the details of our human experience until we are blue in the face, without ever having the clarity of mind to see the real issues we must address before we can even *begin* to have real happiness. These issues are global, not individual ailments in a world of peace, but individual *awareness* of a suffering human world.

The denial, the unwillingness to be sensitive and intuitive, the disturbed value system that we live by in the Western World, all set the stage for the loneliness, the confusion, and the suffering of the children who we like to believe have the best standard of living in the world.

Our children are put through twelve years of schooling in preparation for college. Those who somehow succeed in memorizing the unbelievable versions of human history they are taught, and who devote themselves to twelve years of utter nonsense, will get into a good college. If a child does somehow get accepted to a good college, and is not completely lost in the maze of hundreds of subjects to study, all of them based on the illusions that man has of himself and his world—this child may grow up to have a profession which will earn him enough money to gain recognition within his society. The self-respect children earn through years of trying to prove their worth to a society which values everything *but* what is truly important, can never replace the love they should have received from the whole of society at the moment of their birth into human form.

We are a society which gives lip service to our shared dream of the coming of the Savior, the Messiah, the return of Christ. Yet each child that is born *is* that savior, if only we looked deep enough to see. When the child is not welcomed in the light with which she was offered, she receives the telepathic message "We do not want that which you bring to us," and so she sets it aside and forgets about it. And when she sets aside the gift she brings to the world, she sets aside all that she truly is. For she and her gift are one and the same.

The power struggles going on in all corners of the world, in the form of military conflicts, social competition, and battles between family members, are all symptoms of our feelings of powerlessness.

The most powerful man never needs to fight. He has such confidence, that it never occurs to him to have to prove his strength. It is just a fact. And his energy is so non-competitive that no one feels moved to challenge him. Power struggles only happen between those who have no sense of their own power—and so they are desperately trying to find it in terms of other people.

When the world is at peace, it will be because humans will have discovered the power within themselves. When one knows, without a doubt, that he is infinitely powerful—he never needs to test his power again. The remembering and reclaiming of our own power as individuals, and as a human world will end the need for war. War is simply the way that we, as individuals and groups, attempt to define our own power in terms of an opponent. And we will never find it this way. When we finally discover that our real power has no limits, and is the same shared energy source we all draw upon, we will know lasting peace.

When each living being feels like part of your body, it is hard to turn your back. Compassion is the consciousness of togetherness.

IX

Aborting Abortion

The question of whether or not to legalize abortion should never have been asked. Instead, we should have asked: what kind of cultural life-style has made abortion seem necessary to so many of our women? Could it perhaps be the same belief system and behavior which dismantles marriages? Is not the root of the abortion issue found in the cultural disregard of the sacredness of sexual intimacy, a human joy meant to be shared with one life partner? Might we consider that the role modeling offered to our children does not foster well-timed, intelligently chosen marriages? Has our "use it and throw it away" society demonstrated the kind of commitment where marriages really are a life-long process of individual and couple growth and expansion? Or have marriages been thrown out with the bathwater, as people constantly seek self-esteem and love outside of themselves, in the form of superficial relationships based on physical and ego gratification?

What kind of society views pregnancy as a "problem" to be dealt with? Is not every child a gift? A manifestation of God in human form for the benefit of us all? How can we be anything but joyous! Certainly our society is so disturbed that people still "do not know what they do."

Abortion is a bandaid approach, whereby women are violated emotionally and physically while the real problem is avoided completely. *Our societal belief system does not support the happiness of its members*! So let's change it! No more abortions *please*! We don't need to outline which circumstances are appropriate for the abortion of a forming human being. There are none. Rape is just another symptom of the same societal disturbance which causes us to imagine that abortion is a real solution.

We have violence in our world because we have anger. And we have anger because individuals are so frustrated trying to find happiness in a society which by its very nature prevents it. Of course people are angry. Of course people are robbing banks, killing eachother and themselves, raping eachother physically and emotionally as well as in business—we are all angry. So let's not do this anymore. Let's change. For God's sake, let's change. Because we *are* God, and for our sake—let's come back into love with eachother—come back into the truth. Let's make new agreements. Let's change *everything*! God Bless Us means Bless Ourselves. Let's give ourselves what we *really want*.

When you know who you are, you know what to do.

X

The Most *Misunderstood* Word in the English Language

The root meaning of the word *sin* is *missing the mark*, or *misunderstanding*. When the Christians interpreted the biblical reference to Christ dying for our sins, they mistakenly believed that Christ had paid some kind of debt which was owed due to the accumulation of human "wrong doings." If Christ died for their "sins," then their slate was clean and they no longer had to feel guilty. In truth, Jesus of Nazareth did die for our sins. He was crucified because of *great misunderstanding*. And this is the true meaning of the words: "He died for our sins."

Jesus of Nazareth became an en-light-ened one when he metaphorically threw off his blindfold and saw truth. Never again can one be content with blindness when one has seen the colors of God. It was the desire to share his joy, to not be alone with his vision, that propelled Jesus, as with all great visionaries, into the role of teacher. Teachers are most meaningful to us when they are powerful role models for our own lives. They offer to us a message, a direction for us to find true happiness, peace, and wisdom. What disappointment a teacher must feel when his students, and generations after him, worship him without benefiting from his teachings. Instead of becom-

ing visionaries together, supporting eachother unconditionally, respecting and honoring eachother fully without
judgment—until the last human has thrown off his blindfold once and for all—we debate over semantics, we
power-struggle with eachother politically, religiously, and
socially, and we continue to be unhappy and unfulfilled.

The joy experienced by great spiritual teachers is only
a beginning. Ultimate joy can only be had as a "holy"
experience—literally meaning "as a whole." True enlightened ones know that the only hope they have of experienc-
ing the ultimate and infinite joy, of which they have had
only a taste, is by inspiring the enlightenment of the whole
of mankind. It is to this end that we are driven. In this
highly motivated life work we are, as Joseph Campbell
said so well, following our own bliss. It is not sacrifice or
martyrdom to be a great teacher, as some would have you
believe, but rather the life of one who has seen such a
vision that he cannot rest until everyone can see it together.

Become transparent like air. No one can touch you, yet you can feel everything.

XI

So, What Do We Do *Now*?

"So," one intrigued might ask, "how does one go about becoming enlightened?" I believe that this is most important to be addressed.

The process of enlightenment begins with the true desire. The road to enlightenment is not a lengthy one in terms of human time, but a road paved with commitment.

When one looks into the eyes of each person he meets and sees himself, he is on the road to enlightenment.

When one becomes aware of a voice within herself and chooses to follow the guidance of that inner voice rather than respond automatically to the demanding voice of her intellect, she is on the road to enlightenment.

When one finds himself moved to tears at the most unexpected things, when he feels great happiness welling up within him over "nothing at all," when he delights in simply sitting and watching children or animals playing, when things that used to annoy him now seem very dear, he is on the road to enlightenment.

When her human life seems much more precious because there is so much important work to do in so little time, and when she looks forward lovingly to the day she will transcend beyond her humanness, she is becoming enlightened.

The form he works through to achieve his own enlightenment and to inspire all who come to him, is just costume, whether he works in the guise of carpenter, president, beggar, king, or slave. Human occupations are like props in the theatre. The essence of the story, the message of truth, will come through no matter what costumes are worn, or what names are used.

Ultimately, the desire for enlightenment must be accompanied by trust. One must desire the true vision with such all-encompassing passion that she forgets any concerns she once had about her physical comforts and societal position. In essence, she has faith that the universe will support her as she stretches to grow to her full potential. It takes surrender of what one previously thought was important, complete trust in herself and in the collective wisdom of all life.

In man's commitment to honesty, sensitivity, integrity, unconditional love, and personal responsibility to follow his own truth—he will find enlightenment.

When we make the personal decision to reach across the chasm of our own fear and give ourselves fully to claiming the immense power which is our birthright, we are changing the course of human history. And it is my prayer that you will find it within yourself to meet the challenge.

True power is the falling away of individual identity. Power is emptiness and nothingness, as all definitions of yourself melt away, and you neither begin nor end.

XII.

Welcome!

We are equal. Let me state this again: *We are all equal*. No living being is closer to God than any other. We are all God together. No one is more God-connected than you are. We are all equally sacred expressions of God. This is not just an inspirational idea—it is our physical and non-physical reality.

So who are we worshipping? Our religious leaders are here to remind us of who and what we are. If they see the truth clearly, then their message to us is as simple as "Worship yourselves and worship eachother. Worship the ground you walk on, and worship the ground everyone else walks on. Love your neighbor as thyself—but first make sure that you love *yourself*, otherwise you're not doing your neighbor much good!"

Sadly, some who proclaim themselves to be religious leaders would have you believe that they are more God-connected than you are. These religious leaders would have you believe that all humans are *not* equal, that in fact there is only one phone line to God—and they own it. And good human beings who have lost touch with their own higher awareness fall prey to this kind of confusion and manipulation. The true healers and spiritual masters are those who have achieved ongoing peace and joy in their own lives. They are the few who recognize their true identities, and therefore recognize your true identity as well. Their most powerful offering is to be like a mirror to the world, reflecting to all the sacred God-expression that each and every living being truly is. True healers and spiritual masters simply remind us of what we already know, but have consciously forgotten. Looking deeply into the eyes of a great teacher, one finds humility, acceptance, joy, humor, and unconditional love of all life.

There is no life form more appropriate to worship than yourself. For none are more important, nor more sacred than you are. And when you can *feel* the truth of this, when you can see the sacredness and the beauty of all that you are, you are beginning to understand the sacred beauty of all other beings as well. The ecstatic experience of surrendering to happiness cannot be put into words. There is simply a vibration rising within you, making you want to cry and laugh at the same time. There are no words to describe what one feels when one is overflowing with the incredible, infinite feeling of joy bursting with love, and love bursting with joy for the marvelous, wonderful, miraculous *all* that is—except, perhaps one word: Welcome!

Afterword

I envision a world where work is simply the natural creative expression of each individual. I envision a world in which humans honor and nurture eachother's creativity and individuality. I see for us a world where business ceases to be business at all, and instead becomes sensitive, supportive human relationships where our creativity and love manifest as physical comforts for everyone, without sacrificing the beauty of our natural world. I imagine a world in which labels are set aside and people describe their life work, not in terms of one word, but in the context of sensitive descriptive dialogue. Idealism would no longer be a word which evokes long sighs and rolling of the eyes. Instead, idealism would be the very seed from which all our creative efforts are born. Sarcasm, anger, and feelings of hopelessness would be something that we read about in history books. In their place would be awareness of our true needs, sensitive and clear communication, and committed agreements which are honored as sacred.

Glossary

Heaven—An altered state of consciousness, where one no longer experiences herself as a separate entity, but identifies simply with the all.

Happiness—The feeling of love vibrating in your body.

Anger—A power source we generate in response to not being fully loved. When accompanied by honesty on every level, anger is the fuel for expanding into greater understanding. With greater understanding, one looks back and realizes that the one who did not fully love him was none other than himself.

Ego—A state of amnesia, where individual expressions of God identify with their physical forms only, and therefore experience all other God-expressions as being separate physical forms as well.

Physical Form - An artistic expression of a great artist. In choosing to take on this form, the artist enjoys a multitude of vivid physical and emotional experiences in the context of an infinite painting full of individual characterizations and expressions.

Pain—Physical and emotional experiences which are of a very intense vibration. Are sometimes associated with important life transitions or events. Can also be symptoms experienced when, in physical form, we have forgotten who we really are.

Love—Depending on your state of consciousness, love can be many different things. In its highest form, it is a total heart connection to all life. The most profound love is paradoxical, an intimate compassion so accepting of all things that it may seem like detachment. Love is a heart vibration which is quietly ecstatic and loudly peaceful. Love is something you cannot see. But you can see its action. In that way, love is like God.

Judgment—An experience where God expresses as more than one physical form, and the physical forms relate to eachother in a way where some expressions are seen as being wrong, and some expressions are seen as being right. This kind of relating stems from the illusion of separateness. Ultimately, very little can be said about judgment, because to deny its validity—would be to participate in it.

Language—Tool for loving communication, or barrier to intimacy (your choice).

Reactivity—Behavior which is determined by external events and one's own cultural conditioning. One feels like a victim of outer circumstances, and relates defensively to her situation.

Responsiveness—Behavior which is empowered, responsible, and thoughtful. One chooses the most loving, empowered relationship to external events, knowing full well that he is not separate from them.

Bibliography

The New Testament, translated out of the Greek 1611, revised 1881, Oxford at the University Press, London.

Marcus Allen, *Tantra for the West, A Guide to Personal Freedom*. Whatever Publishing, Mill Valley, CA 1981.

Eileen Caddy, *God Spoke to Me*. Findhorn Publications, Moray, Scotland 1971.

Ken Carey, *Terra Christa*. UniSun, Kansas City, MO 1985.

Alexandra David-Neel, *The Secret Oral Teachings in the Tibetan Buddhist Sects*. Maha-Bodhi Society, Calcutta, n.d. Published in the United States by City Lights Books, San Francisco, CA 1967.

Ceanne DeRohan, *Right Use of Will, Healing and Evolving the Emotional Body*. One World Publications, Albuquerque, NM 1984.

Rev. Margaret L. Fling, *Rays of Light*. White Lily Chapel, Ashley, OH 1963.

Shafica Karagulla, M.D., *Breakthrough to Creativity*. DeVorss, Marina Del Rey, CA 1967.

Max Freedom Long, *What Jesus Taught in Secret*. De Vorss Marina Del Rey, CA 1983.

Yen Lue, *The Secret of the Golden Flower, a Chinese Book of Life*. Commentary by C. G. Jung, translated into English by Cary F. Baynes, Causeway Books, New York 1975.

Stephen Mitchell, *Tao Te Ching, A New English Version of Lao-Tzu's Original*. Harper and Row, New York, New York 1988.

Ira Progoff, *Jung, Synchronicity and Human Destiny*. Julian Press, NY 1973.

Michael J. Roads, *Talking with Nature*. H. J. Kramer, Tiburon, CA 1987.

W. L. Rusho, *Everett Ruess—A Vagabond for Beauty*, Peregrine Smith Books, Salt Lake City, UT 1983.

Helen Schucman and William Thetford, *A Course in Miracles*. Foundation for Inner Peace, Tiburon, CA 1975.

Henry David Thoreau, *Walden*. The New American Library, New York 1942.

A. J. Ungersma, *The Search for Meaning, A New Approach in Psychotherapy and Pastoral Psychology*. Westminster Press, Philadelphia, PA 1961.

Alan W. Watts, *The Way of Zen*. Pantheon Books, New York 1957.

Alan W. Watts, *The Book: On the Taboo Against Knowing Who You Are*. Vintage Books, New York 1972.

Alan W. Watts, *Cloud-Hidden Whereabouts Unknown*. Pantheon Books, New York 1973.

About the Author

As a youth, the author studied Jewish history and comparative religion at the University of Judaism in Los Angeles. She went on to study art and anthropology at California State University Northridge, and two-dimensional media at Art Center College of Design in Pasadena. Very interested in human perception and expression, she returned to the University of California to study human behavior. It became clear over time that all subjects offered at the University were profoundly related to each other. She began to understand that science and religion are man's way of seeking truth and meaning, and ultimately God. Maya Sarada Devi earned her Doctor of Divinity degree in 1988, and became the founder of the Sonoma County Institute for Psychospiritual Growth and Well-Being in Sebastopol, California.

The Sonoma County Institute for Psychospiritual Growth and Well-Being was born from the philosophy that all human interactions are opportunities for personal growth. Stress and depression are common symptoms in our modern industrialized society. The S.C.I.P. Institute's purpose is to alleviate these symptoms through counseling, teaching, and the establishment of intentional communities around the world.

Sonoma County Institute for
Psychospiritual Growth and Well-Being
Box 978
Occidental, California 95465–0978

(707) 874–2001